Gnashing My Teeth

Gnashing My Teeth

poems

Colin Greer

Lantern Books | New York
A Division of Booklight, Inc.

Lantern Books
128 Second Place, Garden Suite, Brooklyn, NY 11231
www.lanternbooks.com

Design by Jens Jensen

Printed in the United States of America

Library of Congress Control Number: 9781590566152

ISBN: 978-1-59056-615-2 (paperback)

ISBN: 978-1-59056-616-9 (ebook)

Contents

To Owen, Sasha, Skye,
Maya, and Cosmo:
the next generation of legs

Foreword

by Robert Powell, PhD

Our contemporaries, unlike people of previous times, generally tend to show a remarkable lack of appreciation for poetry. Yet, as Colin Greer points out, poetry has the power to awaken our imagination. A true poet has the ability to harness creative imagination. Rather like an artist painting a beautiful or meaningful scene, the poet "paints with words," creating a vista in the imagination. As Colin Greer indicates, the faculty of imagination is rapidly disappearing in our time. He, as a poet, feels called to apply himself—by way of poetry—for the awakening of the imagination as one of our most important creative faculties.

The poems of Colin Greer have an edge to them that awakens our sense-ability to imagine and feel with him what, on a deeper level, he is seeking to depict. In the first part of this volume, his poems traverse Old Testament history in a very modern way—biblical themes set in modern times.

After his "Calvary" poem, he leads us into the post-Christian era with poems—again in his unique modern style—that touch upon the New Testament era, one referring to the Apostle Peter and another to Paul. Thereafter this cycle of poems departs from the preceding biblical/historical foundation to explore a variety of life experiences and themes, with the clear goal of awakening the reader of this poetry to see beyond experience or the historical theme to another level of reality—each poem offering vignettes of the author's varied life experiences and probing mind.

To describe the poetry in this book as thought provoking—albeit true—is too weak a characterization. With this poetry the reader becomes acutely aware of the plight of the modern human being seeking truth and meaning in the unfolding weaving of history and in daily life experiences. Colin Greer helps the reader in this quest, showing the way forward through his penetrating honesty and directness. The poetry presented in this volume has an awakening and refreshing quality.

Robert Powell has an enduring passion for the stars, and was awarded a PhD for his contribution to the history of the zodiac. He is an internationally renowned lecturer and author. He is also the translator of the classic spiritual work *Meditations on the Tarot*. Visit www.sophiafoundation.org and www.astrogeographia.org. Robert is the author of numerous books on star wisdom and the divine feminine, Sophia.

Acknowledgements

The legs in the cover photo belong to my children (almost thirty years ago). Talk about believing in the human spirit! Always my great loves and perennial seeds for my creative energies.

My wife, Frances, is the gardener, she radiates from a core of loving intelligence. How else would the seed flourish?

Thanks to Gene Gollogly for wanting to publish this collection.

Great thanks to Robert Powell for his foreword. I have read his wonderfully poetic translation of *The Meditations on the Tarot* so many times.

I also want to thank Rebecca Erwin for her assiduous copyediting and insightful comments.

The arc of history
Swings on hinges to close.
Sometimes it remains ajar
(anonymous)

Introduction

"I Had to Believe It to See It" (Yogi Berra)

These are poems. So in an introduction to them I can talk about belief. I want to talk about belief and imagination, what I believe roils in us, and how we imagine what we feel. That's what informs these poems...mostly in indirect ways. So some transposition might help: the core beliefs I bring to bear here are not ungrounded in scholarship, some anthropology, archaeology, and personal recognition (which I hope the reader will share) are at work.

The unseen driver of our troubles, the rot in our beliefs, the curdle in our imagination, is quietly destroying you and me. What is it?

The answer is "scarcity"—defined as the experience that we never have enough. Scarcity is woven into the way we do almost everything. So long as we are subject to it we will never have enough because means to secure health and love will always be regarded as scarce no matter what the supply is like.

Indeed I believe wired into our epigenetically evolved reflexes, in our social and physical relations, is a scarcity unconscious located in our unconscious psyches. Studies of Stone Age economics confirm what religious texts and psychoanalytic studies have told us: that even at times when material goods were plentiful, the high prevalence of infant death meant that bonding with the mother was delayed until there was a strong likelihood that the child would survive. This may have led to very young children habitually longing for an embrace that never came.

We know that in ancient times it was not uncommon for parents to delay naming a child until life seemed to take hold. We know there were affluent parents who turned to wet nurses to preserve shape and survival. Bonding has not been a guarantee by a long shot. Over generations, such infantile longing has become the leitmotif for our cultures, driving a sense of scarcity into our perceptions, expectations, and institutions, never to be satisfied. This may explain why CEOs of our companies seek more and better pay packages when they currently earn more money than they can ever spend. Maslow's hierarchy of needs suggests that once our basic needs for food, safety, and shelter are fulfilled, we can move onto higher things like love and belonging, esteem and self-actualization. However, the sense of scarcity trips us up and means that we think that five-star hotels and limousines are part of our basic needs.

Millennia of experience have been transmitted over generations of lore and law, intravenously addicting us. Pursuing such junky delusions of necessity and survival means that we are constantly in 'hunter' mode—seeking more and more material resources. And yet, both archaeological and anthropological studies of hunter gathering peoples show that the gatherer mode accounted for more of the food supply than the hunter mode. This means that the collaborative relations of the women gathering were equally if not more critical to community wellbeing than the bond between the male hunters. Yet, it is the hunters' paradigm that has come to dominate our approach to our social systems, leading to hierarchies of power and privilege. So, while the wholesome qualities of collaborative relationships are central to social equilibrium, it is the scarcity-based mores and conventions of the hunter mentality that continue to dominate.

This trans-historical survey suggests to me that scarcity is both prehistorically given and historically reproduced in social systems and organizations. As the scarcity engine runs a constant search for new wealth, this, in turn, leads to rampant inequality, shrinking of character, and soiling of the soul. The consequences are that eight people own as much as the poorest fifty per cent of the world's population.

Religious devotees and seekers after meaning and truth have found ways of downplaying ego, taming the desire to conquer and win, and conveying dignity on all people, while treating our planet with the care and respect it deserves. The French Revolution, the Enlightenment spirit, called for Liberty, Equality, Fraternity. Not just one of the three. We've tried that each in serial systems. They were, I believe, meant to be taken together. A tripartite equation for better angels to fly right.

We know that it is imaginable and that we've fallen short. We know that the hunter hero dominates our admiration hierarchy of reward. We cooperate of course, but we don't lionize that drive. Can it be that cooperation is more than an arrow in the quiver of survival? Perhaps it's akin to how our brain skills developed because we could imagine more. Therein may lie its true purpose or, love the thought, we might be able to determine purpose free of the scarcity unconscious stranglehold.

There's a challenge. Thank the Lord for poetry.

Theodor Adorno framed the challenge in his book *Education After Auschwitz*. Adorno expresses deep concern for the "coldness" that humans so easily resort to in meeting others distanced by race, religion, tribe, etc., and made easier and more likely by technology (clear to him by 1930!). Auschwitz, he claimed, came from the mind freezing over. Given (not inevitable) wiring makes our *exhortation to love* (to warm up) all too often paper-thin. James Baldwin put it in this way: "People are trapped in history, and history is trapped in them."

It's not simply about inventions, nor simply about political and emotional curricula. This warmth Pitirim Sorokin (he studied love, odd for a sociologist) claimed is an active force that can be mobilized for good. The x-ray vision of our moral intelligence must see that marvelous inverse potential and grow it. Recall your Newtonian physics: an equal and opposite force is needed to change the trajectory of a moving object.

That was Walt Whitman's dream:

> I dream'd in a dream, I saw a city invincible to the
> Attacks of the whole of the rest of the earth;
> I dream'd that was the new city of Friends.

But without a deep wellspring of authentic and unconditional warmth, bonding...love as the priority of our lore and law—that is, our best intentions are always provisional and can be undermined at any moment.

None of these beliefs, oscillating between intuition and speculation, has directly shaped a single poem; safe I am in obedience to W. H. Auden's command: *thou shalt not commit a social science.* But these are the contours of my thinking and conscious quotidian concerns as I've written the poems collected here.

Prophetic Voices

"Truth is electrical I've heard.
Could it always have been
Turned on and off
With a switch?"

(anonymous sage)

All in the Family

Booba said *shanda* a lot
When the outside white stone stairs
Were muddied and bruised.
The same *shanda* if my parents
Closed their sweet shop in 1940
Two years after buying it
Just because Hitler dropped bombs.
Shanda if a Jewish child married
A non Jew. People looked like stairs
But there was no cleaning or scrubbing
After that.
Booba spoke pigeon English
Never knowing a pigeon is a dove,
Or birds are dinosaurs.

Coin of the Realm

Back in 1973 or so
                    When ethnics followed their bliss
As hyphens of Americanness
            I thought: This is the tender of the U.S.
The difference between value and worthlessness.
On both sides of the coin is a picture of slavery
Not visible, slaves are not visible typically
But a kike and a nigger, minted historically, perennially
To be spent freely in crises of finance and confidence
Through sexual zigzags, inflation cadences
Black and Jew return the highest interest
Long after the pyramids and cotton fields have passed.
The simpleton asks if we are cut, or cut down, do we not bleed?
The naïf asks what a great question, what should I read?
While bones char and pikes rust
The busker sings "In god we trust."

I want to write about being Jewish
From inside this house that's down
To its studs and joints.
You can see fractured wood and chipped metal
Load bearing   still load bearing
Grass growing underfoot   not a house
But I can imagine building a home here.
I'm looking for an architect who understands
War in peacetime   avalanches on flat land
Barbed wire woven out of hay
Which is a look that has a following.

Understands construction on quicksand
Knows about how windows, attics, and basements
Can link to underground railroads
Wagon trains   river boats.

I want to write about being Black
But I'm not Black. I wonder if
Being Jewish serves.

Gaslit

He lit the gas to make tea.
The gas or the tea or both
Got him thinking: *I prefer gas*
To electricity. I survived it,
After all.

Don't trust me, he said
His voice as brittle as burned toast.

He stared at me in a kind of dare.
His suffering was supposed to be mine
In his recipe book. He was not empathetic.
Nor I. He cared less. I cared less.

He poured the tea for both of us
I was steeping.

Mezuzah

The message is faded or not.
Not is significant
Not is life to be lived.
Not faded
          With a kiss
In passing
          in and out.

If the ink is thick I can
Yell at the guy reading his smart phone
On the tread mill
If its faded he'll probably
          Kick my ass.
That's empirical
          Nothing mystical.
Nothing mystical?

          With a kiss
In passing
Into the therapist's office
Who is not Jewish (rented from a Jew)
If the ink is fading
I needn't go in,
If I knew that was the case.

Instead buy a coffee in a store
With a neutered doorpost.
Leave a 30% tip on $2.30

Drop a dollar on the smelly man
Who opens the door.
If the ink is thick
        He won't touch my hand
As I drop a buck in his.
If it's faded
        I'll get the flu.
That's empirical
        Germ theory.

It's Halloween
The man at the door stretches out an arm
To pry it open
        Half a crucifixion pose

He's wearing a Trump mask   rubber
I notice
I don't care
If the ink is thick
        He'll take off the mask
Tomorrow
        Throw it out.
If it's faded he won't.
That's empirical
        Or bashert.

Prophets and Commandments

Not all commandments are made equal
Not all prophets have hindsight ***and*** foresight
Leaving their perches at the dock
As seagulls do when boats return to their moorings
In summer.

The smartest prophets
With a singular instruction on the tips of their tongues
          Keep their mouth shut
Knowing how gnats swarm with rising tides.

Some are tailors.
They sit where they can
          And sew carefully
A sock down at the heel
A pantaloon cut loose by winds.

Ham's Lament

After forty nights at the helm
He bruised the dove.
Dancing to the fire in his brain
He saw only a pigeon by another name.

I cover him with a blackened red kilim
Rougher to touch than I expected
He wakes to find a print that matched my own.
Snarling, he shakes his Winchester at me.
Or is it a Golden Boy .22?

I see the lightening erection of his shame.
But then he hangs my picture on his wall.
Oh. No, it is of my brother, not of me at all.

Cain

The longest suicide note in history
Is being written by a spotty boy
With long fingers
Gripping white steel.
Angry, brain swelling angry
Because his siblings have more pimples than he

He weaves smoke in circles
Into history's longest suicide note.
When his parents showed him pictures of Einstein's
brain.
Fourteen pictures, he spent fourteen days
In target practice
Until bulls eye.

He thought about
The circular repeat of it all.
What went on between himself
And other people.
A little bird whispered "cog" in his ear.
He could feel what she meant
Every time he fired
He wrote the longest suicide note in history
In the air.

Abraham and Isaac

Alone with his son
Abe scratches the scroll of the dead
With his gun.

The dark of summer
In hill country
Arrives gradually
Like cows grazing a last sup before sleep
Or a child searching for one more
Game not quite knowing
He has no fizz left.

Abe watches night come in
As he watches the child
With wonder and impatience.
Sarah's mirror
Cracks her mind,
Shatters her face,
While god shivers

Isaac and Rebecca

I have been standing for hours
Waiting…
I see him coming as I wait.
He is shortsighted. He doesn't see me yet,
So I wait
As I have for hours.

He'll see me soon, recognize me:
The moon rules when the sun sets.
And I wait, ammunition hidden
Until it's time.
When he speaks I will answer.
I will hear my voice for the first time.
He has the fuse I have been standing
For hours to ignite.

Leah and Rachel

When Leah lost Jake to Rachel
She heard nightingales croon to her sister.
Then they chirped to her:
    "You have one wish," said one
    "Ask for rubber bullets," said the other
    "So you can bounce back."

Leah prayed for rubber bullets. She also
Wished Rachel no good gut wrenching pain.
She and her sister labored.
Leah's boy was older…
                    Leah bounced back.

Joseph

It wasn't fair.
I promised
No part of me
              to her.

O brother
Brother
You live inside a rotten barn
Rocked by rats.

O brother
Brother
Let me build you a boat
To sail amid the stars.

O brother
Brother
If you fear the dark
You know only how things seem.

Gunpowder and lead
Her husband loads half moon clips
Laughs me wrong

O brother
Brother
Bite your tongue
Soon your neck will wring like a bell
O brother
Brother
Bow your head.

Moses

To dislike "dislike" is human.

If the Lord told Moses
Jews will get long noses
(unto the generations).
Shazam, homiphilly!
  big noses look alike
      small noses look different

To dislike
      Dislike!
Is human.

Aaron told Mo and Miriam
"You're missing something
Your lisps are not pretty," he said.
Moses took his broom handle Mauser
Out under the hot sun
Until Exodus burned like Etna.

Miriam's Cup

Five days alone with cactus and cramps.
Moses spoke up for me.
I saw myself in the princess by the river.
My tongue was as metallic as a rifleman's rifle.
Not shrill and thin like my mother's.
You can see Aaron's shyness in his eyelids.

She heard when I spoke for my brother.
She could tell I did not cut corners.

The master gunsmith makes me whole.
God's face turns to me.
I can see the face of god without squinting.

Joshua Fit the Battle

He blew his horn
(got it from a ram).
Filled it with powder
Blew jazz outside of Jericho
Blues, too, until
Hemlock filled in the air
Up and down the killer hill
On which the city stood.
There was so much crying
It looked like rain.

David

You brought me to the perfect thing
A blinding beauty to my bed.

You brought me to the perfect thing
I put a cannon ’oer her husband’s head.

As I crushed the angel’s wing
You kept me from the perfect thing.

Barbed Wire

I vow to value what I have
Anything,
except barbed wire
Tastes good
With mustard and sauerkraut.

My white teeth won't crunch,
yellow teeth will
then they splinter.

I hate barbed wire
More than ever.

There are those who buy barbed wire
By the roll,
There are those who roll it,
And there are those who pass by.
I never liked barbed wire.

When I close my eyes I still see gun smoke.
They bleed. I cry blood.

I never liked barbed wire,
I hate how it grows.

Vanity all is Vanity

(Song of Solomon)

I met history
Like the Scarlet Pimpernel
Rescuing aristocrats
With a Winchester
Pissing in his pants

I met history
Parading like a gunslinger
Behind a closet smile
Feeding a magazine

The wind blows

I met history
Running headlong into a bullet
Dancing to the music of time
Always a foxy trot, syncopated
On full moon clips

No one knows who blows it

Then I met the future at a bar
By the dock where I walk at night
His head bleeding like a broken inkwell.
He was charming
Really knew his wine

Or where it's from

I saw the nozzle at his sleeve
He said a lot I forget.
I recall the walnut stock, and
The wine.
I'm sure we must have made a date
To meet again.

Or where it goes

In the Lion's Den

The gossip in the court was that Daniel
Had swallowed a rat.
    Overnight he lost thirty pounds
    His ebony skin looked paper thin.
    The lions were thinner too,
    As if from disappointed expectations

The gossip in the court didn't reckon
On the angels that guard heroes.
With Benjamin Tyler Henry or Evans.

But the sultan saw the rifle writing on the wall.
He saw the moving finger.
While Daniel was signing autographs
for country girls
In line
to run their fingers through his curls.

Samson's Rash

For the rash on Samson's neck
Doctors sent a nurse to administer
          tincture of myrrh
Which did not help.
But a taste of her did…

Until he saw god differently.
Until his hair weighs on him.
The full moon clips are duds.
He needs clearer sightlines.

Her sweat flaring in his nostril
Lingers…
Working like a semi-automatic silencer.
Meanwhile, she is driven by another love
Than the one she has just found.

Deborah

Her husband held a torch for her
They both knew she needed light
To see leafy palm trees.
Now she could see a thing or two:
How to look at a colt and remember
She could turn the driest clay to mud.

Samuel the Judge

Samuel recognized the child. He watched the
boy wince, sweat stinging his eyes. Samuel
took the boy's right hand, his aged mother let go
of his left. She sweats too, from the heat in the
kitchen. On Friday mornings the kitchen burns.
It remains hot until the women cease their work.
Men repair to the synagogue, and anybody who cares
about the world prays for its repair. But the kitchen
cools slowly and like young David, even grown ups wince,
sweat stinging their eyes. Philistine soldiers
never eat with their families, they sweat blood
in battle, their magazines mix an intoxicating cocktail.
On the Sabbath the women try to
hide all the cherries they can find in the ark of the covenant
Or in other secret, unnamable places.

Samuel was a discerning man. If it takes a king and a gun shop
So be it. He heard the beating drums grow loud
Then louder. Amid the din he recognized David.
He watched the boy wince from the sweat of his labor.
He watched the boy build a temple of stones,
And with uncanny alchemy turn each into a bullet.

Elijah

This should be Jerusalem, but it's not.
Is it the African in me like Augustine
Who wants confession to mean surrender?
There should be light but there isn't

Maybe this could still be a good day.
I arrive to find my background checked.
So I drive my car to the ferry,
crank the rearview. It's up to me.
Time to be the captain, not the crew,
Anti-aircraft, anti-tank, anti-ship.

Repeating cannon, gunpowder and lead,
Broom handle Mauser.
Have to have tools to grow back what's
Been lost for so so long.

Southeast of Eden

Alley oop! Comes along a somebody.
She remembers she is nobody.
She meets another somebody with a better
Memory than Hannibal's elephants.
She still remembered
Abel's shoe out there in the snow.

Adam is bored with the dull force of
His desire. Eve covers herself fearful of
His snores. The serpent sucked
On his tail, Adam sucked on Eve. Abel's
Shoe sunk deeper in the snow with every storm.
Eve could see this but she was faint from mourning.
Like his father, "more" was his middle name.
Eve had taken up arms against her sea of sorrow
Now, she lives by the rifleman's creed:
"I am a survivor!"

It was the third day of the second decade
And who was she to say it was not good.

Calvary Re-mix

He gave thanks for the truth
And lived
(It's been called resurrected).
Who now remembers
He was protesting crucifixion.

His voice was shrill when he gave thanks
As if he were calling
In a forgotten love dialect,
Giving thanks for the truth.
Hanging up his guns
He sounded like Lincoln
Imagining freedom.

When the Cock Crows

A farmer
named Simon, née Peter
When he heard his cock crow
Twice, took two stripper clips
With five rounds apiece.
The animals scurried hither and yon
To escape the bloody feathers falling on them.

Paul

He bought a derringer from the store
Across the street from his favorite diner.
He wanted some thing new
Not old soda with a new name.
He knew it was a phony,
No real fizz. He considered hunting
Forty days and forty nights
But he chose a trip instead.
On the road he took a fall
Which sprung a well with the
Sweetest freshest taste of all.

Jubilee

1300 was the first papal Jubilee. Leviticus called for it
long before.
Free slaves, cancel debt.
If only.
Instead calls to prayer and pilgrimage on a
credit card.
This time, maybe next, the crowd will be washed clean
Including all the debt for this trip.
There is always such a great wailing.
Folly I hear it called.

In 1300 Jubilee spread like a fan. Epidemiologists
Would say an insect caused it.
A precocious child might ask: how can an insect cause
People to do that?
A simple child might ask: who made the insect?

On the Run

"Beat the drum
    with one drumstick
There is only one.
Watch for potholes
    where there were stones
Charge up the battery
    of your torch
    or the fog will
    keep you from home."

He bled as he wrote
In stained letters
Which ran with him.

"Desertion maybe is
    suicide
Is not desertion,
            your call."

I pinned his poem
To my wall.

Jonah

If they ask me
I'll say:
    don't ask.

If they ask do I?
                I will say:
Is the Pope old?

If they ask will I?
I'll say
Does a pistol have a trigger?

When they rail against me
I'll take a train
    When they trample on me
I'll take a boat
    When they toss me aside
I'll float.

What's Ninevah to me
Or me to Ninevah?
Let me float.
I'll float.

Tower of Babble

The body politic legislative body
of work
          body language
          mind body babble body

A body needs a roof
                    body of laws
                              of rules
Canonical embodied

Confidence authority
                    submission
                    body armor
Gnawing other bodies
                    as it advances.

The flow of mastery over other bodies
                    swelling
                    as it advances.

Fallen bodies non fallen bodies
                    of water
oceanic feeling…
More than a notion

Psalm 137

1. The guillotine's ice sharp blade on its way down.
   Is beautiful in its way
2. A street beggar wishing you well as you hurry by
   Is beautiful in its way
3. A marksman who can shoot a hole in a man's head at a
   great distance
   Is beautiful in its way
4. Using Clorox or confession to clean house and move on
   Is beautiful in its way
5. A driver who breaks hard to spare excited rabbits
   Is beautiful in its way
6. A bound felon who studies law and recites Rumi
   Is beautiful in its way
7. When the glue never loses its grip
   Is beautiful in its way.

Nachson

Johnny's given name was Johann
His mother called him John
His father called him Sean
Because he was all "skin and bone"
Johnny called himself Nachson
Then jumped
From a tree into the river
He knew the trees from way back
He always knew how to jump
It was his great skill
From childhood
He always landed on his feet
He walked for hours afterwards
Trying to step out of the mud, trying
To understand what his body just knew

Naming

Giving things their names
By their qualities
The man and woman in Eden
Would be *dumb*
They would be *gullible*
They would be *shaky*
In the wind of the devil's breath
And the surprising farts they blew.

A child could not count on such parents
Running around naked
Seduced by each other and everything
That stepped in to break the boredom
Of their repetition. Cain was no surprise:
Angry kid. Abel licked ass.
Rebel and conform to name some names.

A Why Sandwich

Think: why

Thought: a Jew's harp has no predictable pitch
its wildness is stolen
from a mad Samaritan.

Write: a Samaritan was robbed
by a semblance victim
with screwtape cunning
leaving the Samaritan in distress.

Wrote: insects defend their young
with what they defecate.

Written: a comprehended god is no god.
That's St. John walking walking walking
in sundried AD Constantinople.

Thought: a Jew's harp has no predictable pitch.
it's found, in some shape and form, everywhere.

Think: why?

Lilies of the Field

Reason is transfigured by any will
That rides it.
Truth is not in a judge's sentence
Or policing that locks it up.

On a city balcony 3' x 5'
The dusty world percolates.
Boeings and Airbuses swarm
Like pacified bees not yet
Looking for more succulence.

In the wheelhouse cockpit ships bridge
Whatever
Hackers slovenly hammer into systems
Codging a next meal.
The wired rascal code of centuries.

Reason truth hacking hammering
Lilies of the field
And weeds
Crabgrass finger grasses sticking
It to LED hydrangeas.
Tell a veggie farmer you find bindweed beautiful
You can leave.
Forget you've only been talking about
Morning Glory.

Tea Time

It was hot when two women invited Mary Magdalene
To tea outdoors.
Both sit on metal chairs by a ceramic top table.
The Madonna in the gentle curl of a swan's neck
As she stretches up up and down.

The becoming friend took no sugar
Drank earl gray for the first time.
When she spilled a little due to her stone arms
The ladies took the damp cloth as a shroud
The echo of a sacred blow delivered al fresco.

Stone is not always unfriendly. Sometimes there's water in it.
Sometimes it rolls to free the dead.
Mary is still, her cup is empty.
The women are grateful reassured black tea
Would have been a terrible idea.

Gnashing My Teeth

I walk along the beach   kicking doubt
About like sand.
I hear fish pucker their lips
To laugh at me   remembering…

She, Eileen, lay tephilin 3 or 4 times a day
So much she said because god made a terrible mistake:
I pray I can become a husband and a father.

We were friends. She was beautiful
I was sure underneath she would be
A wife and a mother.

The rabbi's coldness
Like arctic frost on rock
Left us both shaking
Like calf's foot jelly.

Eternity ad infinitum

"What matters?
Who knows?
Everyone asks."

(overheard after a philosophy lecture)

Dorian Gray through a Looking Glass

A flag waves frayed strands darkened
By urban fume. Still it embodies a woven
Cleaner spirit.

While "Les Baigneurs" grow crotchety and wear
Pajamas the brush strokes and colors look brighter
Than ever.

An old couple hobble in the park tired by sunshine.
But tucked in bed in the dark they cuddle so
Canoodle fires their dreams.

A child's dog grows old and lame yet
Their heart links abide on a finer grain.

Long after my parents died I swear they looked
Younger in their photos than I remember them
On a Margate beach or dodging traffic on Cambridge Heath Rd.

Easy to live moulding, full of sell by acquisitions,
Prepackaged assets that diminish our vision and our belonging.
They shape our stride and our fashion while
In our cellar portrait we may be growing prettier and prettier.

Gentrification

The high street coffee shop has been sold
And reopened under the golden wings of the bird of prey
Spread out in gothic arches. People come and go
Talking mostly about the new nail salon
And the four wheel drives they buy
To get through to parking in the snow.

Good is Gold?

Silence is not golden it's rusty
Base metal.
Hold your tongue? Really?
Try thinking holding your tongue.
Try talking with your tongue
In your hands.

Silence is not golden not if
You want to live among others. Even dogs
Appreciate a kind word. Spoken word
Is not like light, its life span
Is shorter. ETA is soon.
Form follows function asap.

Silence? Button your lip?
Like wearing a coat to the neck
On a summer 90°. Discernment!
If you can't say something nice Really!
Scream fire if you see sparks fly,
If you're choking on smoke.

Irreality

I forgot my password and I refuse another.
Maybe my fingers will remember. They have played
Scales for a long time. I won't opt for another number
After the last one took me and lost me.

There is no I in it. No reflection, no image
I recognize in words and letters I didn't intend.
How can another code provide what this one hides?
How can another name not simply do the same again?

Take me and lose me in a modern game
Of hide and seek. Hide from the bully pulpit throne
Elected ruler censor. Seek the bully's softer under belly,
The wider seat and a place in line indexed preferential.

In a game of honor thy father and mother
Duking it out at the OK corral of podcast amnesia
Telling why other fathers and mothers were felled.
When a password was a number pinned or branded on.

When they came for 1772 I did nothing. I was a different
Number. When they came for 2653 I was silent. Afterall
I was a different number. When they came for 3675
My number, I had forgotten it. But they had not.

Jerusalem

There's a song: I don't like anybody
Very much. And there's ancient teaching
Warning other people are not shadows
You are not alone real.

We walk 9 stations
This is where Jesus tripped
Scraped his knees, women comforted
Him with tears tearing the heart out
Of the stone pavings. There are marks.

There's a shy bird hovering over
The tarpaulin cover of the market
I see a right wing flutter
Like a woman with a hand on her hip
Carrying vegetables. She scratches her elbow.
Her funny bone is amused by me.

In the courtyard of Emporia
I see a rabbit perched on a prayer rug
Like David watching Bathsheba on a super-hot
Day like this one.
The old paint on the paving wrinkles
Cracking stones
Like dry skin.

Then station 10: people eating hummus
Hands touch across the service counter
Sharing tables with strangers and familiars.
A cry goes up: The best hummus in the world!
Laughter shakes the old lighting like phone wires
    in a crowded city.
Even the sun casts no shadow here.

Melville in a Time Machine

Quaker City bound for Jerusalem.
The sun burns its own kind of reality.
I'm told even angels dislike strangers.
Ambergris pooled in the secretion of a big
Fish's gut is mined for prime dons
And prima donnas.
Still the sun burns its own kind of reality.
When Orson Welles spits out Rosebuds
He does not smell so bad yet.
But it is the end of Citizen Kane.
Meanwhile coffee aboard
The Starbuck would not be amiss.

~

A boat sails towards the horizon
I'll call it a trawler
To give you a picture of it
A wrong picture. If I say
It's a tug boat you will have another wrong picture.
Like a red doll called blue
Or a black doll called boat.

On the Spectrum

She wears a hard hat
Over her mortar board.
She reminds me of a schizophrenic
Groundhog lost so in her shadow
She can't see it. So Spring and Winter
Oscillate on the spectrum.
After years in a cave with a match
And some twigs.
She gasps as they pass laws
To criminalize matches, fearing
Someone might burn down a barn
To catch a rat.
If you're angry
                Clap your hands
If a homeless lady claps in a forest
And no one else is there does she make a sound?
                Do trees listen?
Do trees have ears to hear?
                Do trees have hearts?
Leaves are wilting... like the eyelashes
Of an abandoned baby
                Letting go of hope.
                Do trees have hearts?

If you're angry and you know it
                Clap your hands:
It's a natural experiment.

Philosophy 101

A jazzy counterpane supports us
As a parachute might if we were
Falling from the sky.
The window guard keeps the kids
Inside. When they are grown
The rail keeps the past safe.
You tell me love is not an argument
I don't have to count the petals or
Stack them by color. *How can*
You grow grass on asphalt? I ask.
You tell me there are saplings
Sprouting hungry to put 2+2
Together.
It's a different point of view. You
Insist love is not an argument.
I insist anything that matters is.
We are not crows.
There is no straight line.
We lie there and snooze
It's going to take a dragnet
To open your eyes she sings
In a lullaby melody she composes.

Sardines

Sardines
Meet in cans
Before the tight parking
They never get this close.
Smoking is a dolorous process.
The fire burns through
The skin which was how they signaled
Each other.

Except these who come in public chains
For breakfast
Who thinks about the inner life of sardines?
I first did. Don't know why.
O yes
The plastic.
Ocean flotillas of plastic
Make trawlers look more like
Sheep than lion.
And then the fire.
And then the cans.

Scenes

Who Pulls the String

Tea leaves compacted in a bag
Cannot be read. Sometimes I miss the strainer.
The string is always a surprise
Like a mouse in my cup
Who pulls the string? A waiter might.
I might. Something to ponder
While I drink my tea.

Hot Surface

Hot tar melts the surface.
My car jack sinks into the ground
Like pride in quicksand.
The spare smirks at me.
I can see it…
In the turned up corners

Scaffolding

Scaffolding is a blessing in heavy rain.
The kind of rain that will make
Dog shit swim. Otherwise it shrouds
The sun bringing dark down too soon.
The man in the moon says: call me "they"
But the pine platform mutes "their" sound.

Sirens

Street sirens bleat like robotic sheep
Their electric minors intimating terror:
Where is the shepherd for these lost lambs?
Sound passes before anyone answers.
Pedestrians walk a little more slowly
Cars making up time drive a litter faster.

A Man

Beware the splinters of broken glass
Beating retreat into sinking sand.
There is no spile to be found.

A whale of a man, Mr. OrCah
Limps like a dog leashed to a biker
To tread clear water.
Camera shutter clicks. Passerby blinks.
Inner life suborned into evidence in public.

Secrets of the Universe

1. In the scullery of my mind
Hiding under tarpaulin
A murder of crows
Prefer not to eat each other.
I am an easier target.

2. It's dark when the ferry docks
Rocks are barely visible.
This is like a great secret of the universe:
We know.
Even so, we trip and break our backs
Like a metal rail requisitioned
For alternative service.

3. Can a body be requisitioned?
If so, who can do that?
I mean, by whom?

   Can a body be coded
Like marmalade, indicating sugar content?
I mean, how sweet?

   Can a body scorched by being brought to boil
Cool down, reach a right temperature?
I mean to say, can it survive?

4. April is the month I begin to reclaim
   My dock from the seagulls. I read
   On Tyranny: So when it rains
   I blame the gulls. When it's too hot
   I blame the gulls. When the IGA
   Closes at 7 not 8
                  I blame the gulls.
   Shunned, pariahs, sent to Coventry
   I tell them: "Spring is mine sayeth—"
   Or I recognize another great secret
                  Of the universe:
   I know to look out for shit on the planks.

5. I often hear myself talking like "101
   Things To Do When the World Falls Apart"
                  So Medieval
                  So ecclesiastical
                  Such biblical sweep
   Like: If you love freedom, release the strands
   You hold of other people's bondage. The friend
   Of your enemy does not have to be your enemy.
   War disguises cruelty as virtue. Reset everything
   With a rib-crushing embrace. Don't try to grow
   When you are trying to sprout.
   101 like that.
   Should be 102:
   Watch out for the seagulls and the crows.
   Or 103:
   Look out for the shit on the planks of your dock.

Skin In the Game

I wake up worried
late, I get my coffee and toast
Annoyed at how long it took to make.

I'm taking a shower.

What's with the water pressure today?

I smell mildew in my towel My lungs hesitate to breathe,
It's got to stop.

I'm writing about
gang rape and pov-
erty in the Bronx I'm
afraid I'm going to
miss my deadline
I'm frustrated about how slow I type,
Coughing on cigarette smoke coming in from next
door.

Deadlines like
this make me

wish I was dead.
It's got to stop.

The heat is full on

and it's August.

I am gagging on the rancid
mustard in my Reuben sand-
wich. I've been trying to reach
my trainer

To postpone her for today.
She reached me, tells me
It's all the same to her. She adds:

She's been thinking about rape in the Bronx and has some ideas.

It's been a busy week

She knows that's lame

Neither one of us has

Much skin in the game.

Still Life in the Late Afternoon and Evening

A crumb on the floor
Captures me
Like a memory of a food taste
Digested past
Not forgotten.
Clean it up, I tell myself
Straining between the fifth and sixth
Thoracic vertebrae
Not allowing my chest to expand
For a crumb
Not forgotten.

Jazz on the radio
Churning in the radiators
A water tower reflected on a neighbor's wall
Like a girl waiting to dance
All the world in the orizon of my eye and ear.
Sun tires
TV pundits hum the dance electric
I hear a toilet flush upstairs.

Still life in the late afternoon
And evening.

Thinking about "The Sea and The Mirror"

(*W. H. Auden*)

Might Lady Macbeth have become Miranda
If Prospero had not destroyed his books?
Might Oliver have chased away Charles the assassin
Not hired him to kill his own brother if Prospero
Had not set Ariel free?
Might Edmund have cherished his father
Defended Lear if Prospero had not left
Caliban to rot?
Would Henry have defended Falstaff
Visited him on his deathbed if Prospero
Had found Trinculo in his bathtub
And splashed about a bit?

Thinking About You Not Me

What is kindness?
Can it be a gesture like yours?
You know how you are? Is it
A character quality? Or a
Device like a rocket shaped storage
Container on the top of my car?

Is it helping a blind person cross
The street, you know the proverbial?
Or just not tripping her because she walks
So slow. Or is kindness like a grey wall
That doesn't crumble when weather stains
It with darkened spots?

Someone said kindness is a work
In progress like a poem that won't finish.
Like a garden hose on
A timer. Depending then on some
Outside force that keeps the turn on
Switch from rusting in the rain.

Blind Spot

A three pronged thought sticks me
In the back of my eye
Where the ganglia collide to limit perception.

The homeless people I pass on upper Broadway
Are cripples, craggy, and crooks.

My eye hurts
I blame them for the pain
In the muscles of my blind spot.
The boggle my mind rejects
My eye feels.

Lear was blind. So too Othello, Hamlet
Macbeth, Faust
        Crooked craggy
        Crippled.
Samson was blind. Solomon, Peter, Constantine
        Craggy crippled
        Crooked.
The blind spot always hurts
The prophets felt it.
What is a prophetess to do?

Empire

Empires are clouds
Dreaming up and dressing down
They reign they stop
They rise and dissipate.
If you consider speed of light
There is a duel pending between Herod
And Putin. Blind as war / eyes bloodshot
Opium from Outer Mongolia through isthmus and
 channel.
Cows blow methane and iron fillings from smithies and
 trains
Magnetized to the cortex.
The clouds rain screws and stars
The stones cry.
That's what such clouds do
As they rise and dissipate.
That's what they do.

Eternity ad infinitum

Tamburlaine's turbulence was well known.
First signs: shook his shoulders to bring his shirt
Sleeve below his jacket cuffs. His costume cuff links
Catch a glint from the overhead neon. Electricity
Crackles above and below, converging in him.

His wife paces behind him. She looks less tall
Behind him. In front she's taller. She carries
Twins in her arms and a newborn on her back.
All three are too big to be carried.

Tamburlaine has bested Neptune. He carries 3
Holes in his head in a row. He paints
Animals on wine glasses in his blood, pigs
Cows chickens. He paints the heads of horses
On the carousel in Neptune's blood.

Tamburlaine's turbulence rises and falls
In tides of despair, in mudpiles of broken promises,
Hopes drowned by the loss of children to the sea.
It was said his last wife died at the beach
Drowned by water poured from a bucket by a rebel soul.

He built a country house on that very bay
With no electricity, no outhouse. His new family
Shits in the woods. His new wife wipes his new
Children's asses with leaves from a 350 year
Old oak tree

Tamburlaine can belt out a laugh in the woods.
Louder than Joshua's ram's horn. His post nasal
Drip requires a bullet sized spit to clear his throat.
Surrounding the hut unseen are those who live lives
In darkness perennially. Their king and kingdom
Is their reach and the cover of trees.

To the lives lived in darkness Tamburlaine's family
Means nothing. His laughter is meaningful as
Is the night. His sound is full of light. So
The dark lives suspect the hut. The lightness
Of being in it.

Tamburlaine dreams of despair. He
Tries to laugh but there's only silence in this
Dream that feels real. Is it the past he dreams?
The imminent future? Is he missing something?
When he wakes he quickly attaches his pigtail.
His black pigtail.

The brown pigtail carries the meaning of joy. The
One he attaches this morning carries the meaning
Of war. He feels himself filled with anti life.

He steps out. He is on the road to
Tar sands which fills him with a new species of hope,
Hope with centuries of half life ahead. This is a new
Caliber of longing.

Tamburlaine remembers he knew both Lamarck and Darwin.
Their fathers and mothers were in his court
Before they themselves were born. He knew what
They had to say: that something about change he hated
To think about. Fast and slow it was all the same.
Loves, hates, befriends, defriends from day to day.

The guru he had known living in a pocket
In a coat in a closet encouraged him to laugh. Just
Laugh! In his 98% unused brain, Tamburlaine
Felt no reason to laugh.

The sun of suns which he used to confuse with himself
Has become a tired wish.
More in the range of despair when he considers
Laughing. He prefers to sleep. Courtiers find
That unacceptable and nudge him with the tip
Of his sceptre.

This equilibrium lasts and lasts. He remembers
He has 98% of his mind to use. He squeezes
Through silence where there is still no longer
Laughter. His second family stays in the country.
The lives in the dark eventually capture them.
Sell them for the light between their pores.
Tamburlaine can't scream. Instead he insists those he
Conquer scream before they die. He builds
An encyclopedia repertoire to ensure screams
Happen.

The pimple of recognition on his own skin
Itches most afternoons. Without distraction he
Is an irritating mess. He decides to return
To the road, to the tar sands. This time
His ponytail falls off when he swings it at
Mosquitoes.

Tired. He finds his hut, his empty hut.
He sighs a deep sigh. He has only his story.
A way to share his certainty that justice is not imminent.

Fezziwig

Mr. Fezziwig
Comes and goes
Just like Jesus, dead at 33.
Fezziwig was middle aged
But his time in Christmas Carol is short.
He was crucified.
The golden rule melted down
Do unto others
And poured into the shape of land mines
Wrapped in paper money.

Goldilocks and Yogi Berra

She bites her tongue
She tastes blood
She has blood on her toes
She stares
She examines her feet one at a time
Lines criss cross her soles   life lines
Tarot   Ezekiel's dream.
She thinks he's staring at her.
She winks.
He returns the gesture.
You have to believe to see, he said
Anticipating Yogi Berra.
She limps
From an old bear hug
Where she found timelessness.

Out of Many Voices, One

When heat turns to lightning
When backfires turn to massacres
When trees hang low in mourning
    Not in prayer
We have something to expiate
    More than Lawrence and his snake
    Bigger than Orwell's elephant.

But still my heart leaps up
    Like Wordsworth's
When I behold rainbows
On the street.
When lions lie down with lambs
    (as they do on occasion)
Sunshine on the water.
My grandfather's Woodbine cig succulent
In the case I bought him
On the Isle of Wight.
    Like Sonia Sanchez
We revive the beauty of forests and winds.
    Like Baldwin
We can also ride the lightning.

Stairs

Might as well be a mountain
As I turn the round in the steps
From my apartment to the street.

The marble steps
The concrete walls
Mountain parts

A step too fast
A sorry self-pity apprehension
Of a fall
    Avoided
    A mountain accident avoided
    A day open to adventure
    Avoided.

At One of the Borders

Socrates' flower
In a cup
Hemlock's
Assisted heartbreak
Of insanity
Insisting everyone else
Is wrong
(which maybe).
Then the question that curdles
Like heavy cream:
How different is lonely
Above ground
Or below?

The cobble cracks
A rose strikes a glove
At a hemlock leaf
Red rises
The log on the fire
                    shrinks
                    hisses
                    water drips

Rain has become familiar
                    buckets
                    showers
                    tornados
                    boiling ice

As much as tears are clogged
at the border
of countries
of dominions
A newborn baby boy's father
Trips on his daughter's shoelace
A vulturous braided cuff
Reaches to take it
stretch
it
til soon
For the first time
New to everybody (even here)
A body is lynched

3. *It's a little bit funny*
A Greek song says:
You'll all laugh
In about a week

It's raining
Bread
Crumbs
for the birds.

Organic can food
for the dogs and cats

The rain brought in.

Climate change
Soaking skin
    like blotting paper

Ink in the veins
    mapping the body

Spreading in so many directions
    still so many places to go

For bread
(even for crumbs)

At the Beach

Fustian swim gear is the prude at the beach
Water resistant like a diver's with flower
Design. But the jelly fish get through.
The high pitched sirens are shrill as spitting up blood.
    That would be the work
    Of the inquisitor
Who has an argument
Solid as a colander.

Small price for cruelty
All ermine, light as a heavy feather
Washed three times and wrapped in purple
        That would be the tribunes
Cutting into the semen of heretics
With ceramic knives.

Messrs Cicero Fabius Lentulus
Aka: chickpea bean and lentil
Put up umbrellas to keep the rain
Off the crabs.

Beachers crouch
To throw dice, invest in sand castles
They cower from the sun
Deafened by the sirens in the waves.
        That would be the old men
        Who breathe like fountain pens
        Thirsty for ink.

Gives No Quarter

What is fundamental: if one of them kisses
You lightly on the neck it's an infected affection.

Blind image in the reflexes of no-surrender headlights
On a cliff highway severe enough for commandments to be given.

At one and at a loss
Always urgent sensations: ecstasy and entasy

Hybrid nostalgia   solemn in the style
Of one who is pennywise, low gas battery run down.

On an elevator in a corner as against the ropes
In a ring. *In the other corner:* the oppositional body.

Impossible to say if organic cotton or hemp
Can bind us better. What's between must be more than between legs.
Or else we are free radicals
And who cares...
You can't rent a towel at the gym for 25¢

Permission to Binge

Today feels like we are drowning
In trauma.
        wherever you put your foot down
        you step in it.

The sidewalks look clean enough
But people trip
        all the time
You see them
        scraping their shoes
        on the curb.

x

The moving finger writes
Arthritic by now:
        doesn't matter who survives
        as long as someone does.

Hear the sound of the barn door swinging

Permission to binge?
When the going get crowded
The crowded escape.

x

Relief: channel Langston Hughes
            for a moment
Loving all the rainbow on the street
            the keyboard colors
            holding hands.
I can see Jubilee on billboards
I have a sense
            of rivers he knew
            without invalid algae
            nor unhinged mercury.

It's a Dark Wood

It's a dark wood
Of trees that cower before me:
Are you here to cut?
They must think that
    They must.
Truth is I'm lost
I was never good with directions
I didn't mean to get lost
    So lost!
Lost and angry. In my head a bird
Squawks: so if you're angry
    Clap your hands.
If a man claps in a forest
And no one else is there does he make a sound?
    Do trees listen?
Do trees have ears to hear?
    Do trees have hearts?
Leaves are wilting...
    Do trees have hearts?

If you’re angry and you know it
Clap your hands:
It’s a natural experiment.
Leaves wilt like the eyelashes
Of an abandoned baby
    Letting go of hope.
Does the trunk have enough juice?
    Will its heart fail?
    Will its ears hear?
Metal on metal is deafening.
I could throw away my axe
I could   clap my hands...
    Clap! Clap!
    Clap! Clap!

Political Dispatches

"Virtue and Happiness
Serve well as thought
Serve better as action."

(anonymous activist priest)

Not

Baseball is not America's national pastime
Not the game of those who call the shots
Not the game of by and for those who rule
Those who rule America
  play golf.
Those who own all the teams
    play golf.

Playing polo with shrunken heads
Did Rider Haggard see golf coming?
The Man Who Would be King.
Knowing is always a lagging indicator
    sort of thing.
    u (k) no   w?

2 Cheers for the 1 Eyed Citizen

2 cheers for the 1 eyed citizen
Squinting in the light of a paraffin lantern

I loved a dream which brained me.
My dream was arranged in words.
Recitation impaled me against a wall
Where it was curfew 24/7.
Sun and moon are tied tight in ropes
My dream called herself Law
She took off her clothes, submerged
She shook a sword. Called me:
You think you can make the waves succumb?
Spots broke out all over my body
Which she counted.
What she counts she owns.
People around me in uniform all wearing my skin.

2 cheers for the 1 eyed citizen
Looking for a ride back to Michigan

Still Faithful

She took a bath
Her tricolor wrapped around her blade
Nicking herself shaving her legs.
No excuses
Tired of excuses.

2 cheers for the 1 eyed citizen
Tattooed with an arrow thru "Try Again."

A Short Discourse on Moral Malaise

Adorno asked how in hell (He didn't say hell.
He escaped hell.) Can we hallmark fortune cookie
The world when we forget to lick and stamp the envelope.
And how, he must have wondered, do we rewrite the play
In the great globe one person at a time in time.

Don't make the world a purity test.
Don't wait for the love bug to bite
Before you notice the raisin in the sun
Is your daughter's brother. And remember
To lick and stamp the envelope.

After

What I do best
I mean the best of all I do
And maybe best of anybody else who is good
At washing dishes.
I am exceedingly good at it…
Lipsticked, greasy, leftovers lying after tumescent tastes
I clean up.

I am going to learn to cook
In the republic 'of just in time'
After a narrow escape…
After leaders catch their breath…
After they weep for what they've said and
What they've done
After their wicks are soaked in oil and stagnant rain water
After that…
I promise: I will learn to cook I will do more than clean up
After now…

Alleyways

"It is forbidden to say Allah (or Elohim) in filthy alleyways."
(A religious instruction)

Alleyways are in between
Not always dirty
Encrusted with cobble edges of memory
Forgotten passers thru
                A heel or button lost
In cracks as if there were progress
                Lying in wait after sacrifice.

A mule who shits in a palace garden
Was slaughtered in a temple
And carted to a dump full of magpies
                And canines
Not in an alley but a feast for a rancid
                Insect summer.

Anywhere might be filthy
Moses' shoes might smell
People might raise a stink
A foot can trip where dogs promenade
Payday lenders in the temple
Amazon buying up all the stalls
                To build a warehouse
Filth flies like snow so high
                It could halt
                A battalion
Of conquistadoring chaplains.

Boggles the Mind

Birds over the pond look so lovely
Kayaks glide in the rhythm of spring
Snapping turtles separate as the water eddies
And I am James Comey's shorter brother
In the sense that we are all made in the image and likeness.

When I see a rainbow my heart leaps up
Dogs and subarus know all about love
Canines and motor cars are man's best friends
And I am James Comey's older brother
In the sense that we are all made in the image and likeness.

Oh for a bird's eye view!
Thank the Lord for seeing things up close!
What became of boys like these?
Boys will be boys...

In the sense that we are all made in the image and likeness.

Deportees

Out on the shore you can see the trees miss
Pepe, sap thinning by the day.
Hydrangeas and sunflowers are broken hearted
Maria too left without a word.
The flowers are afraid to console each other
Now that differences matter.
The magistrate said, forgiving my speeding ticket,
You sure look American. We both knew
What he meant.
Phantom limbs whack at the crab grasses
Driftwood figures trim the hedges.
Nothing moves…
Like flowers sinking in a river
Thirsting for rain.
Wood thrushes over the pond don't sing
Te quiero any more. Tropical summers in the north
Have changed their migration patterns.
White Seagulls fish at the shore.

Don't Take the Rule of Law for Granted

Hitler could dance
Wagner had an ear:
Expiatory songs burning
Redemption meter on a pyre
With a gaggle of witches and warlocks.
Replacement sacrifice. Contraceptual
Conjugation! A marriage made ethereal
And lethal. However big the hurt
Don't take the rule of law for granted.

Greedy Corners

In the greediest corner of the garden
A soldier aborts a baby.

A cardinal screams.
Those who enthrall to fetuses
As to god herself
Are silent.

A soldier kills mother and unborn child
Those who enthrall to fetuses
Are silent:

This is war

Just war means sacrifice.

For those who carry life and death
In them
There is no just sacrifice.

And in the greediest corners of the garden
Where cardinals scream
Screaming is excremental.

Inflation

Headlines: 3% unemployment
3% growth no inflation.

Let me tell you about inflation:
It expels a chest so
Puffed even a robin would be embarrassed.
It makes living cost more?
It makes some people think they live
better should live better longer should decide
How long or well others live?

x

I have Mandela's hand
On my wall. A black hand
Five spread digits on a white board
With a charcoal grey border.
Just a hand.

Headlines… by lines…
sidelines…
breadlines…

Let me tell you about inflation
narcissism
greed

Billions in gold on a chest so puffed
Even a robin would be embarrassed
                    at the sound
Of one hand beating on a chest
And another patting on a back

x

Better drive carefully. Don't crush the wheel
You can sneeze into ermine
But it is still snot.

Let him tell you about inflation:
The way a warm breeze squeezes
Through a crack in the window.
                    That way.
The way Mandela seemed to back up
As he moved forward.
                    That way.

Now

Burn the history books. Burn
The history of history books
Burn the tales of the original genius of the United States
Stories of American pioneers
Tales of who invented musical comedy and Murder Inc.
Burn the stories of small town saloon decadence
Gunslingers and madams who could have been nuns
Oilskin myths of slave traders paid for by rich thieves
Banknotes with confessional grills which collect deposits
Saunas, steam rooms, and private jets.

Burn them all!
Burn each page. Tear off the Amazon plastic that suffocates
Every word. Take a shower, apply sun lotion.
Save yourself!
Save us!
The great greedy chain of causation is a nauseating force
Built on myth, misconception, malnutrition of the word
Misanthropy of the heart. Take a run
In the sun. Get some sleep. Wake up.
Didn't Rosa Parks sit down
Didn't Martin King stand up
Check!
Check!
Wake up!
Now!

Polluting the Mississippi

Reimplant ectopics!

They must have shit out their brains
Into the Mississippi and polluted it.
Next they will criminalize diapers
So originary excrement can serve
To sculpt local statues.

Railway Terminal

On track.

"Whatever isn't fascist isn't anti-fascist"
Anti-fascist is a reminder of it all.

"Every crucifixion needs a witness"
Every crime needs a forgiver.

Sign: dogs are not to piss here.
Don't you care?
Not a lot. Anyway my dog didn't.
I saw it.
You saw it wrong.

A cat smells the dog.
Leaps from a window
Breaking glass
Lands on shards.
It would have been her 8th life.

Later train cars rattle over moistened steel
Quickening her dull whiskers.

Sombreros in the Morning

Riding into sunset or the Long Island Expressway
I could be Clint Eastwood or Russell Crow, this could be
The Alamo.

Now it's dark, 475 under headlights is a trail of tears
Trucks like ranchers riding high over steers pound the turf
The moon bounces on cars down the access roads convinced
The earth is flat.

In morning mist headlights shine on sombreros along the roadside
Turned out to be a cold night you can see puddles
Where ice melted.

The Fall

Eden

Adam trips over Eve
She moves a leg to wriggle free.
Her daughter's-in-law can't.
Cain falls under Abel's weight
(The boy loved piggy backs)
There was a flood of tears.

Urban

If only hunger chose another city
If only no one blamed anybody
In the city hunger moved to.
If only those who still ate
Did not gorge.
There was a flood of tears.

Cain again

Cain puts on Wellington boots
To walk in the mud. Then
Running fast through rain
To stay dry.

The Klan

Michael Rogin X-ray vision
Could see scores of men
In gowns and pointed hats
Tossing and turning like
A big white whale burning
The moon off its ears.
To which Toni Morrison
Cried "Amen!"

The Twist of Arms

Imagine words are cup hooks
Cracked by overuse, held together
With 3-M cement in a tube.

Imagine words are skin
Imagine exfoliation . . . free at last!
Peel off the eldritch buildup.
Or buy a Burberry against what's coming down.

Imagine you heard what I meant
When I said:
I hate the sound of blood running
I hate the sound of a cardinal
Bashing his brains out on glass at war with himself

I hate how the great coat is coming undone. I hate
The buttons on the street.
I'm not happy with the button maker.
I'm not happy not knowing who the button maker is.
I hate how numbers keep the bodies hidden
I hate the pretense
And the noise . . .

Orthodoxy
Something like straight white teeth.
Well known by those who crave improvement
Or make routine visits to the dentist.

~

Bishop Tutu offered to pray for my mother
When radiation like rain caught her
Without an umbrella.
He was familiar with Tynedale
Who swung by the neck for the King's English
Without revealing the love part always punches below its weight.
Makes sense Adam's apple got stuck in his throat.

~

The storm was always coming
Everybody who feels could feel it.
No one knew it
Friend's mothers' fathers' children felt it
No one talked about the storm.
They couldn't, no words for it.
They could feel it.

~

I'm told my tears are valuable

But my tears won't be bribed
My towels are soaked
They take forever to dry

Who has that kind of time?
So button up child
Brush your teeth
Wipe yourself

Throw yourself into the twist of arms

~

Bateson said time is human energy mobilized
That makes me cry.

Throw yourself into the twist of arms.

Time Bomb

Four people born every second

Redemption beckons.

She wore a blue and yellow jersey.

She said right off she was thirsty.

She bore two sets of twins in an hour.

In between she took a shower.

In between maybe a minute

240 babies came through the thicket

Breathing thin air

Already sensing nothing's fair

And who cares?

Warsaw Memorial in Riverside Park

1. *The loam of longing*

The longing winds the miles of intensive
Running into clouds
                                        rusting stars
Oak alligators lie in the woods
                                        with birches
They have skinned
                                        opening hues
Under the whiteness.

Bark and moss
                                        miscegenate
Suggesting the neck of a swan.

The loam of longing
                                        hanging like knitting wool
Over a broken nail in a deserted kitchen
Left bare
                                        by hungry soldiers
The loam of longing
                                        hanging like duct tape
On broken bodies.

Isn't it good to know that just a chip
                                        of dry bone
Makes resurrection possible.

2. *Stretch*

Theraband stretch
Once made a man blind
                                        on its rebound
Still somehow
                                        someone
Photographed his iris
And used it to open a secret closet
                                        in Stalin's
Bedroom
Which opened into an apiary
                                        full of bees
                                        millions of bees
In hives
Like Caspian's wardrobe
Freedom is in the air
                                        on either side
                                        inside and out
not inside
                                        it.

3. *Recology*

The art of collecting waste
To retrieve a future:
                plastic bottles
                exhausted hoovers
                dried up Velcro
And diapers
                The seductive future
                Imagined
                Without alms or grace
Like hyphenated migrants
                arrived from the past
Escaping: poverty bigotry misogyny brutality perfidy
                Inventing: railways finance
                                asbestos atomic bombs
                                mercenaries oxy
Or on the other:
                polio vaccine
And who wouldn't drink bottled instead of muddy water
"Give me your…" how does it go?
                Yearning to breathe free.
Or just breathe
Why yes, rummage a bottle or two
                or ID
                or SS #
To eat.

4. *Genes*

Magic School Bus books take kids
on rides
                    Through their bodies
Blood and brain
                    open to train
                              visits
Every stop marked "Elan
                    vital."
Mind in the tender
                    Decoding
Discerning.
Listening I wondered
                    how inside a body
Passengers might be carried
                    from outside
Relatives   friends   stories
                    about family and friends
Who rode buses and trains
                    To destination genocide
Geno
                    cide
Gene
                    structures
Epigenetically composing experience
                    expression
And passing it on
                    copywritten encoding
For a choir to rehearse
                    and release
Perfect(ly)
                    sounding like screeching wheels
Like screeching
                    perfectly expressing pitch.

5. *Poland on my Mind*

Poland on my mind
          fused
with the stone facts
At 83rd and RSD
          of memory
          growing obese
Wild seeds of color blown
          so far off
This iron circle
          is a still life
That simulates the dead.

Is that the point
          of this unkempt grass
          and drooping flowers?

My grandmother would not undress
In front of the TV
          she feared
She would be seen
Best to clothe privately
          don't speak English
People will see who you are
          in the mirror of it.
Stay under the radar
Never show sinew
Never show flexed muscle
Never water
          lest there be flowers.

Is that the point
Of this unkempt grass
          and drooping flowers?

6. *In Between*

A car grinds to a halt
A window blind catches midway.

A child falls to break her run
A father teaches red is not green.

A cul de sac is not a metaphor
A yellow brick road glistens but it's not gold.

Fall hangs on into spring
Spring hangs on into winter

Solstice equinox suntan ice burn
epoch zeitgeist   heaven and hell

A car grinds to a halt
A father teaches green is not red.

Go Home

Lincoln proposed best to return slaves to Africa
To end slavery.
Hitler proposed Jews get out until he changed his mind.
My father was called out to be beaten in Bethnal Green
Go Home. Go back to your country which was Russia
Where lifetime military service beckoned
A boy in shorts
Not yet in pants.

Can a Jew embrace *Go Home. Go back to your own country!*

If history does not repeat the joke:

A Rabbi stood on his roof. Flood water rising.
He prays to be saved. A fisherman comes by in a row boat.
Another then another. He refuses the rescue.
He has faith god will provide.
When he drowns he begs to know why god forsook him.
"Did you not get the memo? Three times I offered"

Then the future will.

Mountain Pose

It was in mountain pose
That I rusted like Creely in worship.
From up there I could see
What disfigures America
My feet shake, my torso turns yellow/brown
Until I tighten my core.
And I do
And I see
America was born mad
And so much of it remains so.
I see.
I do.

It's Been like That

Retail space for rent
Like the mind itself
Pop up   vacuum packed
All the air gone.

The curses coursing through my brain
Blow my mind.
Culpitory steam
Which I reject
Take the fifth.
Who set this up this way?

A wide winged heron wrestles
With a vulture
At the border of kapo and apprentice.
Lazarus taxon
                    Which one?

The dark has been rising
And charging for it.
Like Exxon tax breaks.
What's left gives body to nobody.
Think Arlington as a city of origins
Gnats and ticks.

Who is an oligarch to trust?
His mind must be toothpaste squeezed
Twice a day. No yellow or white lines.

Pigs get fat, hogs get slaughtered
Boys riff on lollapalooza
Girls celebrate cattywampus
Texas is Norwegian for crazy
Don't you know?

Truth is we all have a hitch
                    In our getaway
Words don't mean what they used to
And it was a stretch then.

Ever since snap peas and rice crispies
Sprouted through concrete
It's been like that.

Angel on the Street

A jolly man
        in whites
As if he played tennis or cricket
But played neither
        his whites
Were faded and stained
His belly sat like
        white
Sheets on an elephant's bed
        his white face
Opened to teeth
        white
Polished
        whites
Of his eyes shone like the moon
On a startling bright night
        white bandages
Wrapped his wrists
Made me think he was not as happy
As he presented to me
        in my white
Funk   lost in memories of Queen
Ann lace, vanilla ice cream melting too fast
        white hot
Anger as I hit the street in front of him
He told me to cheer up
Said he was just operated on
        a black surgeon
Saved his life "*man was a miracle worker*
Cheer up life is good
        white man."

Buy Me a Synagogue

When I was seven I ran into a pram
Which chipped my tooth
Growing up is uneven.
I'm not out of Homer or Moses
I don't have a rod that makes rock cry
                    or a mother wince
When she hears her children pray for better.

Here's the one
                    who cut off heads
Over here the one
                    who forced girls to beg for sex
To live one more day.

No one is polite
Not even the panhandler who asks for money
With a grim disinterest.
He's no car salesman
Offers no cosmetic options
No sun shining
through brown grill teeth
Buy me a synagogue for my birthday
After the baby birds have flown
When all prayers fall in like a worn tent
in a light wind.

It's a cold night in hell
No heat in the pipes
No steam to prevent seeing.

MG

Will I ever buy my green MG?

???

Maybe when tires never lose pressure
When hot air floats all boats
When lightening bugs collect robins
In bottles. Or, light up urns
With the possibility of resurrection.

A letter (email) from a friend:
He thinks the world is closing down
On an horizon point.
Not sure, if it's to be reborn or gutted.
He gives it three months
(Hiccups in time, no more).
Could be a terminal calendar.
Maybe the last trimester.

The shepherds are on alert.
The stars bedazzle them:
Low hanging fruit about to spoil
Or saving grace.

???

My green MG would break the sound barrier.
My foot on the petal of marigolds
In the break lining
Put there by flower children
In insurrection mode.

Our Leaders

Walt Whitman asked
In so many words:
Are these the ones to lead
The leaders we have that is?

Everyone's a critic
A comic said.
So sensible
To seek myth and miracles in comics:

Close all the banks
Fingers in the dike
Hans Brinker reflex
Geostorm predicts flash flooding

So Walt had to ask:
Are these the ones
To lead
The leaders we have that is?

Swallow and Repeat

Highbrow mendacity
Is nothing
Newer than a clip-on bowtie
Or a saber tooth claw
Sprouting under an attached collar
On a faded pink shirt.

Airborne toxicity
Is a thing:
It's the thinning forest
Where trees are falling
Like rabid rodents dying crossed legged.

Lies and poisons are twin
Killers: billions of parents
Will die before their children.
(*Nothing worse* sages say)

All these crosses
Could leave the wrong impression:
Crucifixion does not need to be universal.

Still and all:
Take two   *swallow*
Repeat every 4-6 hours

Lest We Forget

This is the Mueller Report
door stopping the entrance to my building.
This is the Mueller Report
wrapping chips in a fish shop in London.
This is the Mueller Report
wiping ass in a power desert in Puerto Rico.
This is the Mueller Report
discounted by 50% at Barnes and Noble.
This is the Mueller Report
stitched on 3 sides to warm the hands
of delivery men
on bikes
in winter.
This is the Mueller Report
less and less than expected.

What Is a Revolution

Pundits say *"god bless America"*
Panhandlers tell you *"god bless you"*
(Whether you give or not)

This is a chaplaincy of the street:
                    "Our prayers are with you.
                    We mourn for your loss."
Deep in the heart of hearts
Who gives a toss?

It would take a revolution.

What is a revolution?
It's not the new chaplaincy of the street
She tells me.
I can feel her palm cup my face.
Isn't it grand how the palm fits?

About the Author

COLIN GREER is the President of the New World Foundation.

He is the author and editor of numerous books on education, immigration, and politics. He also writes nonfiction. His poems have been published in *Transfer, Hanging Loose,* and *Tikkun.* Best known are *The Great School Legend: A Revisionist Interpretation of American Public Education* (Penguin) and (as a contributor) *Choosing Equality: The Case for Democratic Schooling* (Temple University), winner of the American Library Association's Eli M. Oboler Intellectual Freedom Award.

He was a founding editor of *Change Magazine* and *Social Policy Magazine* and, for seventeen years, a contributing editor for *Parade Magazine.* He chairs the board of the Lark Play Development Center.

Two of his plays, *Imagining Heschel* and *Spinoza's Solitude,* are collected in his book *Religious Differences between Artichokes* (Portal Books).

Colin Greer lives in New York City.